# Dear Parents/Caregivers:

Children learn to read in stages, and all children develop reading skills at different ages. **Fisher-Price® Ready Reader Storybooks™** were created to encourage children's interest in reading and to increase their reading skills. The stories in this series were written to specific grade levels to serve the needs of children from preschool through third grade. Of course, every child is different, so we hope that you will allow your child to explore the stories at his or her own pace.

Book 1 and Book 2: Most Appropriate For Preschoolers

Book 3 and Book 4: Most Appropriate For Kindergartners

Book 5 and Book 6: Most Appropriate For First Graders

Book 7 and Book 8: Most Appropriate For Second Graders

Book 9 and Book 10: Most Appropriate For Third Graders

All of the stories in this series are fun, easy-to-follow tales that have engaging full-color artwork. Children can move from Books 1 and 2, which have the simplest vocabulary and concepts, to each progressive level to expand their reading skills. With the **Fisher-Price® Ready Reader Storybooks™**, reading will become an exciting adventure for your child. Soon your child will not only be ready to read, but will be eager to do so.

**Educational Consultants:** Mary McLean-Hely, M.A. in Education: Design and Evaluation of Educational Programs, Stanford University; Wendy Gelsanliter, M.S. in Early Childhood Education, Bank Street College of Education; Nancy A. Dearborn, B.S. in Education, University of Wisconsin-Whitewater

# Ready Reader Storybook™

# Sir Charmer, the Brave

Book 8

Written by Nancy Parent • Illustrated by Pulsar Studio

Modern Publishing
A Division of Unisystems, Inc.
New York, New York 10022

Andrew's class was putting on a play. It was called "Sir Charmer, the Brave."

6

"Everyone will play a part," said his teacher, Ms. Jones.

"Who will be Prince Sloppy, and who will be Princess Neat?" she continued. "Then there's the dragon. Now let me see. Would you like that part, Howard Lee?"

When Ms. Jones was through, everyone had a part except for Andrew.

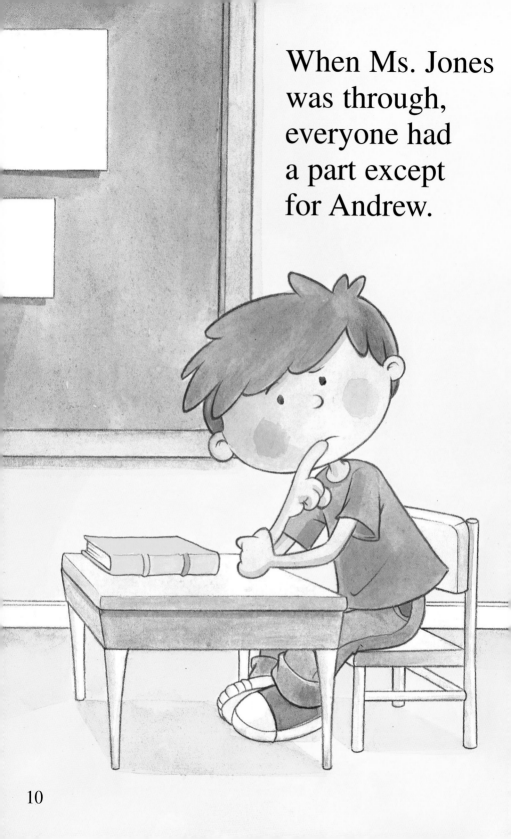

Andrew quickly raised his hand. "What about me?" he asked.

Ms. Jones smiled.
"You can be Sir Charmer,
the brave knight."

Andrew's class read the script for the play.

"This is going to be fun!" he thought. But first he had to learn his lines.

Then he had to practice bowing and fencing.

Andrew liked to walk around in his suit of armor. It was made out of cardboard and aluminum foil.

Andrew's favorite part
was the duel with
Prince Sloppy.

He even got to tame a
fire-breathing dragon.

Nothing scared Sir Charmer.
Nothing that is…until opening
night.

On opening night, Andrew
peeked through the curtains and
saw a lot of people.

His teeth started chattering.
Andrew had a bad case of stage
fright. The play was about to start,
but Andrew couldn't move.

23

"Places everyone!" called
Ms. Jones.

Andrew shook his head. He just couldn't go out there.

"Take a deep breath," Ms. Jones said. "I'm going to count to ten and open the curtain."

When the curtain opened, Andrew looked out at the audience. He saw his parents smiling proudly.

Andrew cleared his throat and began:

*"Welcome to our little show.*
*It's about the knights of long ago.*
*If there's a need, I'll lend a hand.*
*I'm the bravest knight in all the land."*

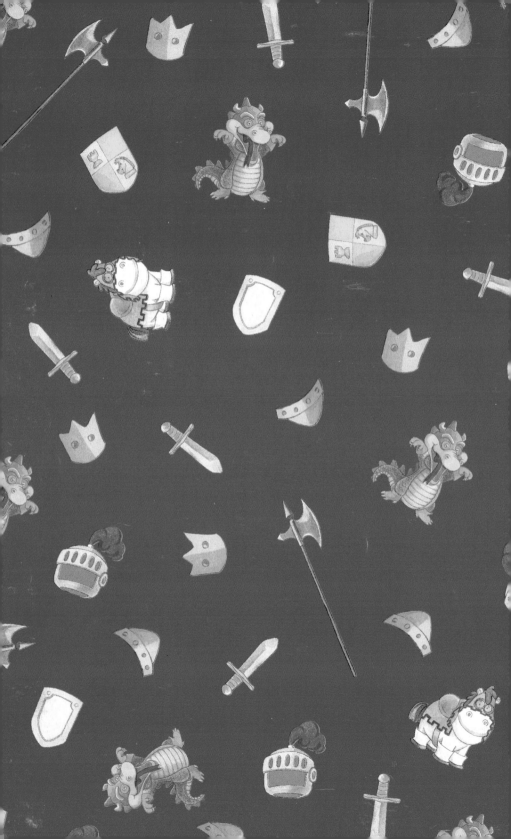